THINGS MEN DO TO *REALLY ANNOY* WOMEN

BY TONI GOFFE

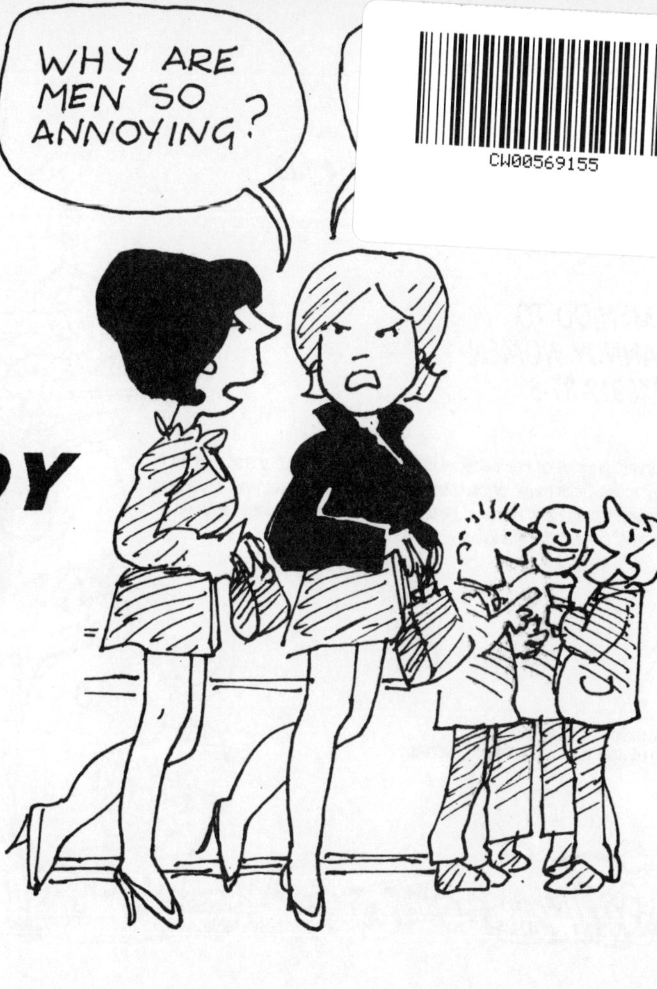

First published in Great Britain by
Pendulum Gallery Press
56 Ackender Road, Alton, Hants GU34 1JS

© TONI GOFFE 1995

THINGS MEN DO TO
REALLY ANNOY WOMEN
ISBN 0-948912-31-6

PRINTED IN GREAT BRITAIN BY
UNWIN BROTHERS LTD, OLD WOKING, SURREY

HOW TO USE THIS BOOK

BUY IT , TAKE IT HOME AND
WHEN YOU'RE SITTING QUIETLY
WITH YOUR PARTNER, READ
IT TOGETHER AND DISCUSS IN
A FRIENDLY WAY WHICH OF
THESE ANNOYANCES APPLY TO
YOUR PARTNER AND WHAT ARE
THEY GOING TO DO ABOUT
THEM?
IF THIS APPEARS TO BE A LITTLE
ONE SIDED WHY DON'T YOU...
BUY BOTH BOOKS...
NOW YOU HAVE ONE EACH.
"THINGS MEN DO TO REALLY
ANNOY WOMEN" AND
"THINGS WOMEN DO TO
REALLY ANNOY MEN".

NOW YOU CAN DISCUSS WHAT
ANNOYS YOU BOTH ABOUT
EACH OTHER.
IT COULD BECOME AN
EXHILARATING EVENING
TO REMEMBER........

MEN ALWAYS TRY TO CHAT YOU UP WHEN YOU DON'T WANT THEM TO...

THEN WHEN YOU WANT TO BE CHATTED UP, THEY IGNORE YOU...

OR...

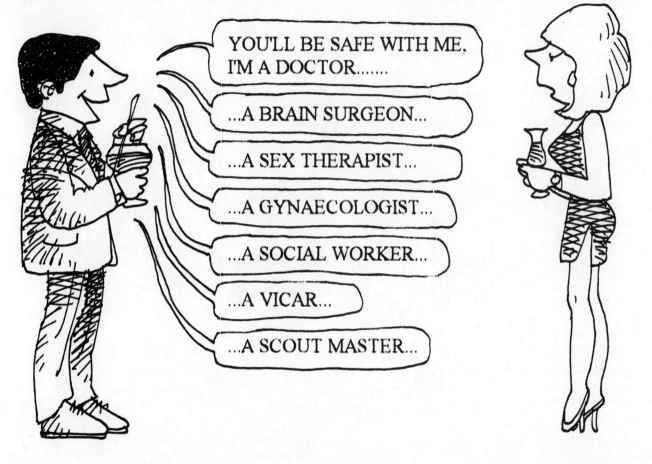

MEN ARE CHEAPSKATES...

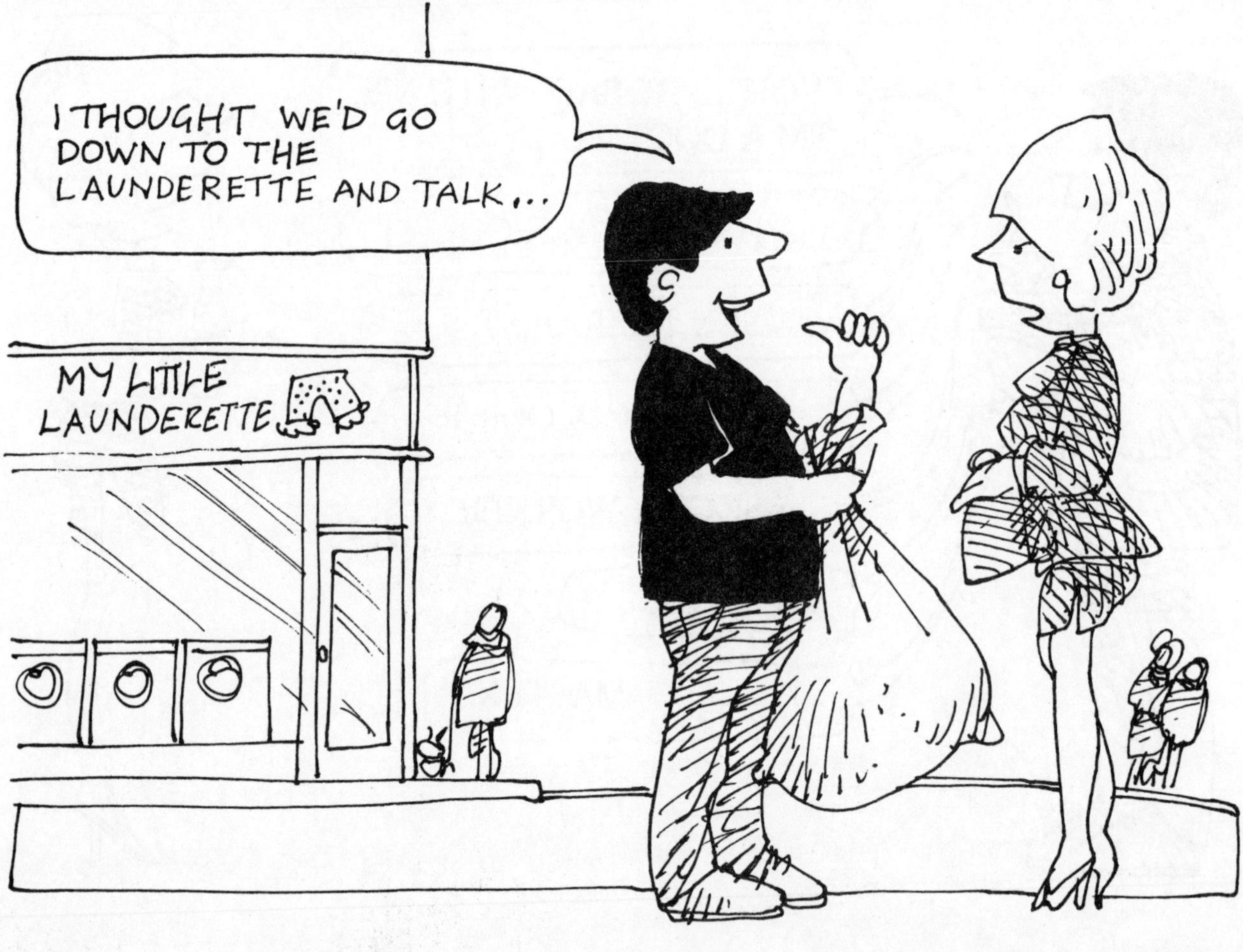

MEN WON'T TAKE YOU ANYWHERE WHERE THEY HAVE TO OPEN THEIR WALLETS...

MEN SPEND TOO MUCH TIME IN THE PUB...

MEN ALWAYS EAT THE WRONG FOOD...

MEN NEVER HELP WITH THE WASHING UP...

MEN, ONCE ON A COUCH, WON'T GET UP...

MEN NEVER HELP WITH THE HOUSE WORK...

WOMEN WANT TO CHANGE YOU AND WHEN THEY CAN'T THEY THREATEN TO LEAVE...

MEN THINK THEY'RE GOOD AT D.I.Y. AND INSIST ON DOING IT!!!

MEN WILL DO ANYTHING TO GET OUT OF SHOPPING...

MEN ARE ILLOGICAL ABOUT MONEY...

MEN ARE ILLOGICAL...

MEN ARE ILLOGICAL...CONTINUED.

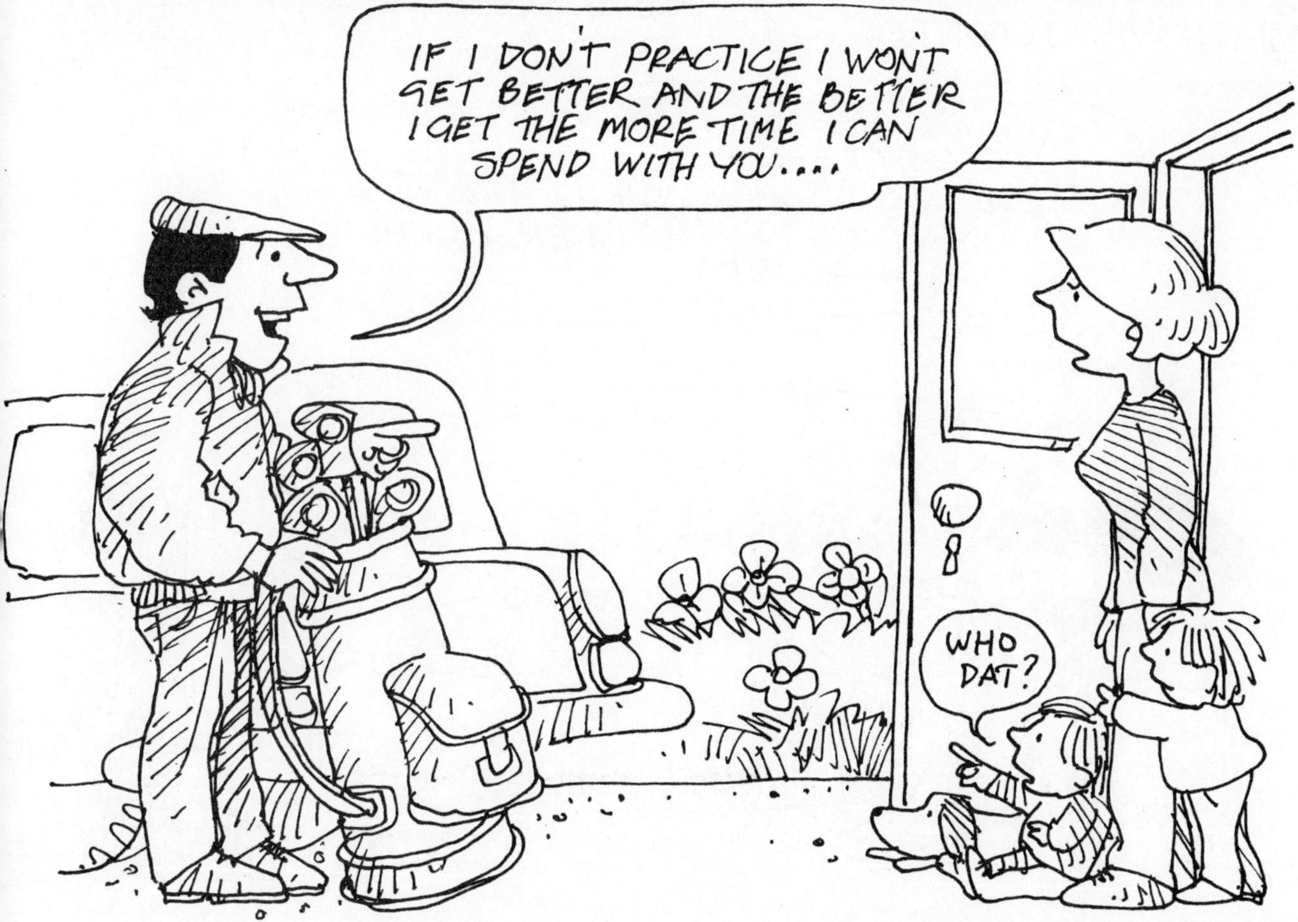

MEN LOVE TO CONTROL...

MEN CAN'T WORK VIDEOS...

CAN YOUR MALE PARTNER DO ANY OF THE FOLLOWING?

SET THE VIDEO...

CHANGE A FUSE...

SWITCH OFF THE ELECTRICITY
AT THE MAINS...

TURN OFF THE WATER...

COOK ANY THING FOR HIMSELF...

READ A MAP...READ A BOOK...
...READ...

DO ANYTHING USEFUL?

MEN HAVE THE MOST ANNOYING HABITS...

...AND THE WEAKEST EXCUSES...

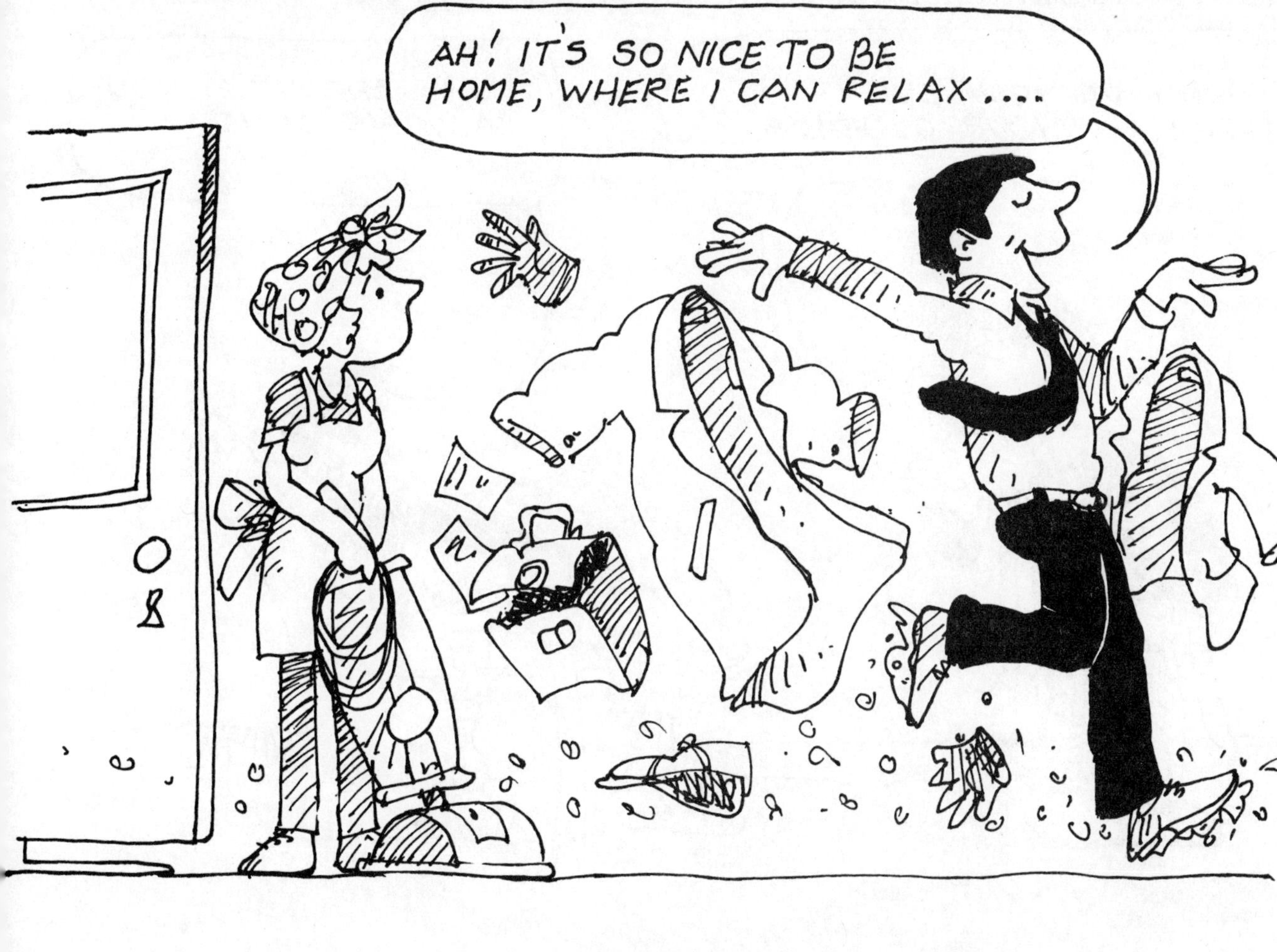

...AND MORE ANNOYING HABITS...

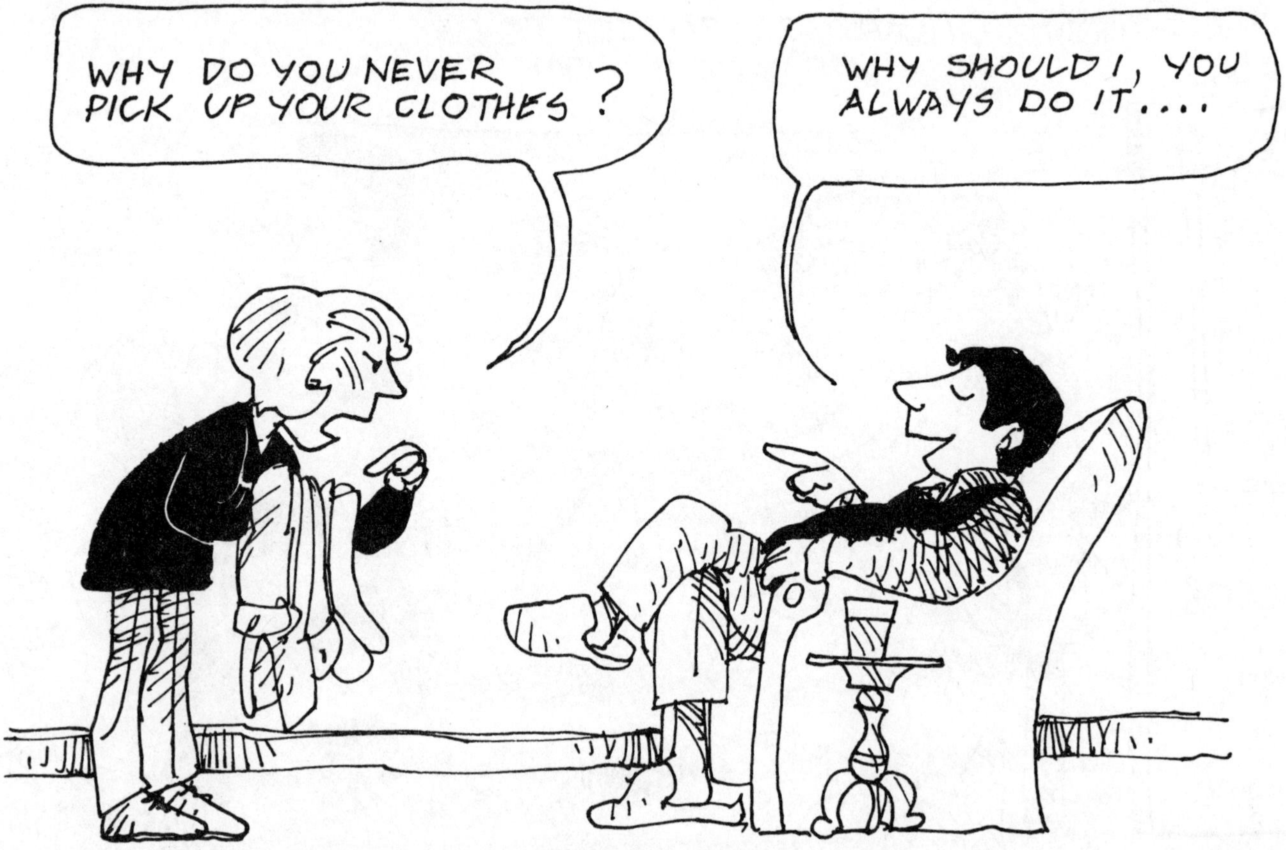

WHICH OF THE FOLLOWING ANNOYING HABITS DOES YOUR MALE PARTNER HAVE?

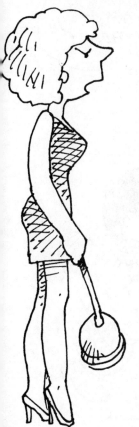

READING THE NEWS PAPER IN THE LAVATORY FOR HOURS...

ALWAYS LEAVING THE LAVATORY SEAT UP...

NEVER CHANGING THE TOILET ROLL...

NEVER OPENING THE NEW SOAP...

WEARING THEIR SOCKS IN BED...

PICKING THEIR FEET IN BED...

PICKING YOUR FEET IN BED...

BLOWING THEIR NOSE ON THEIR DIRTY SOCKS...

SCRATCHING THEIR BOTTOMS AND THEN TOUCHING YOU WITH THEIR SMELLY FINGERS...

DOES YOUR MALE PARTNER PICK HIS NOSE, IF SO,DOES HE ...

ROLL THE BOGEYS UP INTO LITTLE BALLS AND...

PUT THEM IN HIS POCKET (FOR LATER)...

FLICK THEM AT THE CAT , DOG, CHILDREN,
TV SCREEN, OR YOU...

OR EAT THEM...

OR INSIST ON YOU
AND HE PICKING
EACH OTHERS NOSES...

MEN NEVER LISTEN TO ANYTHING YOU TELL THEM...

MEN ARE SUCH WIMPS WHEN THEY ARE ILL...

MEN ARE TOO SELF-CENTRED IN BED...

...AND MORE SELF-CENTRED...

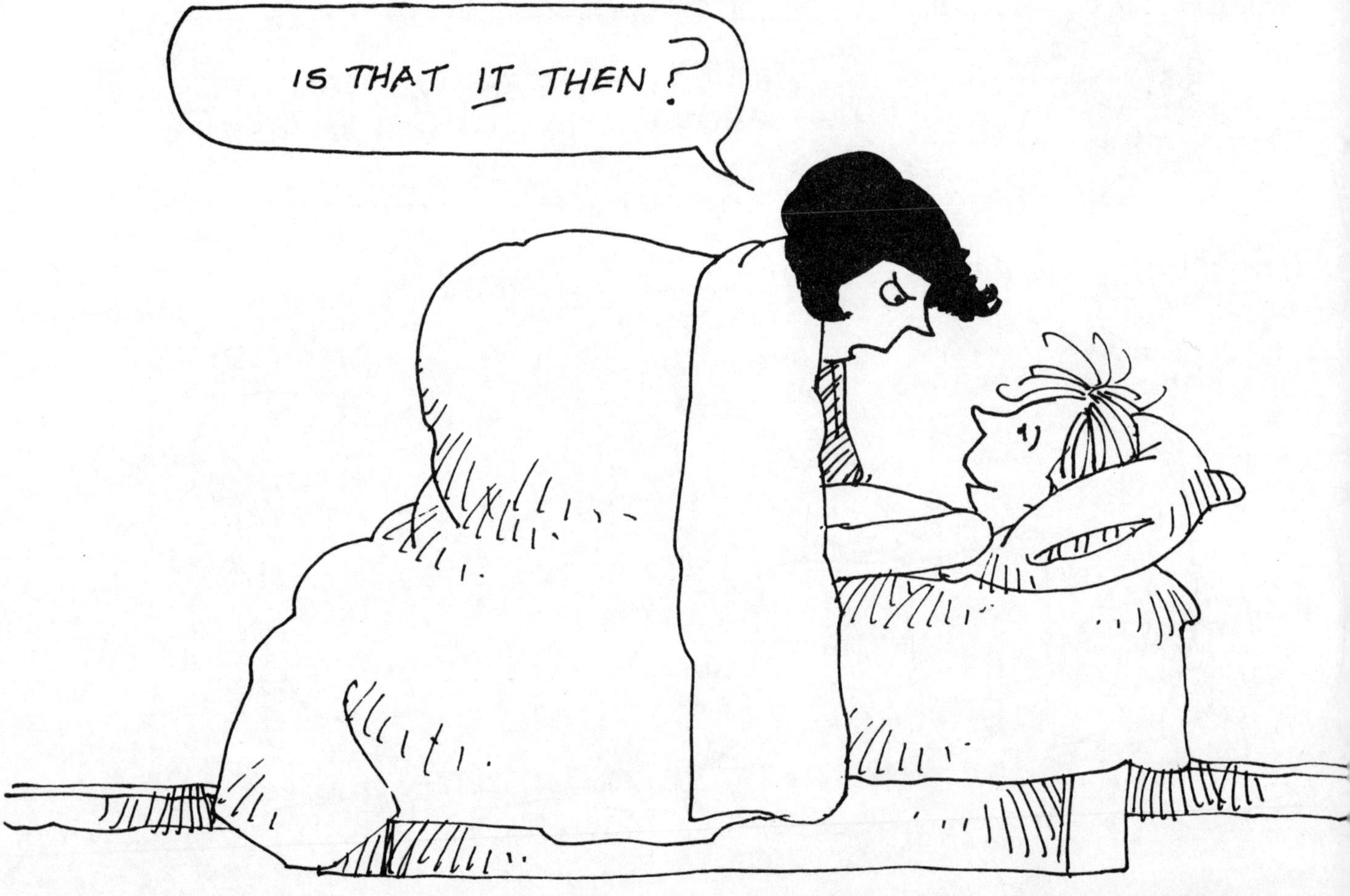

DOES YOUR MAN DO ANY OF THE FOLLOWING
ANNOYING THINGS...

FALL ASLEEP DURING SEX...

MAKE EXCUSES FOR NOT DOING IT...

STOPPING FOR A PEE HALF WAY THROUGH...

GO TO MAKE A CUP OF TEA BEFORE SEX, HOPING
YOU'LL FALL ASLEEP...

BRINGING SNACKS TO BED BEFORE SEX...

EATING BISCUITS UNDER THE BED CLOTHES...

PUTTING THEIR COLD FEET ON YOUR BACK HOPING
TO PUT YOU OFF SEX...

IS YOUR MAN GUILTY OF ANY OF THE FOLLOWING
ANNOYING ACTS?

HOGGING THE BED CLOTHES...

SNORING ALL NIGHT...

INVADING YOUR HALF OF THE BED...

CALLING YOU BY YOUR GIRLFRIENDS NAME DURING SEX...

NOT GETTING UP AND MAKING YOU A CUP OF TEA
IN THE MORNING...

HOLDING YOUR HEAD UNDER THE BED CLOTHES
AND FARTING...

MEN FORGET EVERYTHING...

MEN CAN ONLY DO ONE THING AT A TIME...

MEN ARE IMPOSSIBLE TO UNDERSTAND...

PENDULUM GALLERY PRESS

56 Ackender Road·Alton·Hants·GU34 1JS Fax & Telephone Alton (0420) 84483

SPORT

			IBSN NO
JUDO FOR JUNIORS		£2.99	0.948912.01.4
JUDO GAMES		£2.99	0.948912.00.6

HUMOUR

		IBSN NO
IS THERE SEX AFTER 40 FOR HER?	£2.99	0.948912.20.0
IS THERE SEX AFTER40 FOR HIM ?	£2.99	0.948912.19.0
ARE YOU FINISHED AT 50?	£2.99	0.948912.05.7
ARE YOU STILL FLIRTY AT 30?	£2.99	0.948912.06.5
THE VERY VERY SEXY ADULT DOT-TO -DOT BOOK	£2.99	0.948912.09.X
THE NEW SEX DIET	£2.99	0.948912.04.9
SEX AND YOUR STARS	£2.95	0.948912.08.1
HAPPY? BIRTHDAY	£2.99	0.948912.12.X
HAPPY? RETIREMENT	£2.99	0.948912.10.3
GET WELL SOON	£2.99	0.948912.15.4
FARTING!	£2.99	0.948912.17.0
GREENS ARE GOOD FOR YOU	£2.99	0.948912.13.8
CAN SEX IMPROVE YOUR GOLF?	£2.99	0.948912.18.9
IS THERE LIFE WITHOUT DOGS?	£2.99	0.948912.22.7
IS THERE LIFE WITHOUT CATS?	£3.99	0.948912.21.9
IS THERE LIFE AFTER 60?	£2.99	0.948912.24.3
IS THERE LIFE AFTER BABY?	£2.99	0.948912.23.5
IS THERE A LIFE LEFT FOR GRANDPARENTS?	£2.99	0.948912.25.1
WAS THERE LIFE BEFORE COMPUTERS?	£2.99	0.948912.26.X
WHY WHY D.I.Y.?	£2.99	0.948912.29.4
LIFE`S LESSONS FROM MY CAT	£2.50	0.948912.27.8
LIFE`S LESSONS FROM MY DOG	£2.50	0.948912.28.6
LOVE CATS	£2.50	0.948912.30.8
THINGS MEN DO TO REALLY ANNOY WOMEN	£2.99	0.948912.31.6
THINGS WOMEN DO TO REALLY ANNOY MEN	£2.99	0.948912.32.4

TO BUY THESE BOOKS YOU CAN EITHER ORDER FROM YOUR LOCAL BOOKSELLER OR
FROM US AT PENDULUM GALLERY PRESS·56 ACKENDER ROAD·ALTON·HANTS·GU341JS·
(PLEASE SEND £1 EXTRA TO COVER POSTAGE AND PACKAGING)